Tech Prep
Taiwan-Style

by
Douglas C. Smith

ISBN 0-87367-649-1
Copyright © 1999 by the Phi Delta Kappa Educational Foundation
Bloomington, Indiana

This fastback is sponsored by the South Central Iowa Chapter of Phi Delta Kappa International, which made a generous contribution toward publication costs.

Table of Contents

Introduction

"Education knows no class."
— Confucius

"All national citizens shall have an equal opportunity to receive education."
— Article 159, Constitution of the Republic of China

Prior to the mid-1950s, Taiwan, an island two hundred miles off the coast of mainland China, was considered a Third World society. By this I am suggesting that the economic system in Taiwan was static, that the society was divided clearly into "haves" and "have-nots," and that a high-quality education was available to very few residents. In fact, many young people, after finishing whatever elementary and sometimes secondary education their parents could afford, went to work in menial jobs. The wealthy sent their children to other nations for their high school and college education. Japan, the United States, and less often England, France, and Germany were destinations.

In the late 1950s a transformation began, and since the 1960s Taiwan has reinvented itself as a dynamic, economically energetic, prospering society. Of all the Asian societies, with the possible exception of Japan, Taiwan has been the most successful in redistribution of wealth, development of social plasticity, political liberalization, and expansion of economic opportunity. Today the annual growth of Taiwan is approximately 10%, and annual per capita gross domestic income increased from US$100 in 1949 to near US$12,000 annually in 1997.

The engine for this rapid increase in prosperity was a shift in emphasis from agriculture to industry. But a concomitant shift occurred in education. In fact, one might draw parallel lines on a chart to indicate both the rise of industry and the improvement and expansion of education for Taiwan's citizens. Elitist education did not disappear entirely. Rather, a concerted effort was undertaken to raise the education level of the lower tiers of society, in large part through a "junior college" system that I characterize as "tech prep Taiwan-style."

Roots of
Education Reform

The United States has supported the industrializa-tion and modernization of Taiwan as a strategy to keep the island independent from the People's Republic of China, while at the same time allowing the Commu-nist Chinese to maintain that Taiwan is a maverick prov-ince of mainland China. This complicated political stance aside, Taiwan owes a debt to its Confucian his-tory for attitudes about culture, ethics, customs, and the value of education. The Republic of China is deeply Chinese in character, in spite of its political break with the mainland. Japan, which occupied Taiwan from 1985 to 1945, also was a significant influence on the work ethic and business attitudes of the Taiwanese people.

Education and the economy of Taiwan are firmly intertwined. Thus as the economy has changed, so has education. Some insight into this dual nature of prog-ress is suggested by Chien Liu and J. Michael Armer (1993), who posit three ways of looking at the relation-ship of economics and education:

Human capital theory suggests that individuals with more schooling have higher earning power, find better jobs, and have greater job satisfaction than those with less schooling. Therefore more education equates to greater prosperity for the nation.

Status competition theory suggests that schooling relates directly to the distribution of influence in society. Therefore, as schooling becomes more egalitarian — available equally to "haves" and "have nots" — society itself becomes more egalitarian. This process has an indirect influence on the economy.

Class reproduction theory suggests a Marxist view in which schooling, in itself, is not a determinant of economic prosperity, because much schooling remains classist and thus merely reproduces social distinctions. Transformation can occur only when class distinctions are diminished, rather than reinforced.

In my view, Taiwan's successful transformation is a recognition — and implementation — of the first two theories, which effectively counter the negative aspect of the third theory.

Traditionally, the Chinese have held education in high regard. Those citizens who are less educated have viewed their more educated comrades with respect, rather than contempt. Thus, when education began to be offered more openly, there was a natural gravitation toward more schooling, which begat higher earning power, greater job satisfaction, and so on: the road to economic prosperity as suggested by human capital theory.

The main venue for more egalitarian schooling in Taiwan is the so-called junior college, which has proven to be a stabilizing influence on Taiwanese society. Junior colleges allow Taiwan students who do not qualify for university admission to obtain a higher level of education than was possible only a few decades ago. This access to higher education results in better jobs and greater purchasing power, which, in turn, feeds economic prosperity.

Today a major goal of the Ministry of Education in Taiwan, as well as the political leadership and economic managers, is to develop a workforce that is competent at all levels. Doctors, professors, lawyers, and engineers certainly are needed, but so are computer specialists, retailers, travel agents, accountants, bookkeepers, hotel and restaurant managers, and a host of other, lower-level professionals who can find both economic satisfaction in their jobs and meaning in their social position. A correlation exists in Taiwan (as it does in Japan and most Western countries) between years of schooling and economic success. But in Taiwan there also are numerous examples of men and women who, after completing junior college training, far outpace their university counterparts in economic and financial achievement. The knowledge that hard work and learning can lead to economic achievement works as a further stimulus to the junior college system.

The current level of social mobility and access to schooling has evolved over time, and a brief summary of Taiwan history may be helpful. The Republic of China was founded in 1912. The main goals of the new nation at that time were anchored by nationalism and democracy. A new education system was constructed to support these ideals, but the Chinese economy still turned largely on agriculture. Many people continued to live in poverty and to have little access to the new schools.

That new system, bolstered by talks at Chinese universities by John Dewey in 1920 and 1921, consisted of six years of elementary school, three years of middle school, and three years of either academic or vocational high school. After the academic high school would come the university. But the system, though set in place, never became a reality for much of the population.

Taiwan, which was under Japanese governance from 1895 to 1945, was only tangentially influenced by the reforms on the Chinese mainland. The Japanese and Taiwanese authorities established an education system similar to that found in Japan. Both Japanese and Chinese were accepted languages in the schools, as well as in Taiwanese businesses.

World War II and the Japanese invasion of China brought an end to much of the attempt at systematic education and education reform. At the end of the war in 1945, Taiwan retroceded to China from its 50-year occupation by Japan. World War II was followed closely by civil war from 1945 until 1949, when the Communist Chinese subdued the mainland and the remnants of the Republic of China found refuge on the island of Taiwan.

Thus it was not until the 1950s that any substantial, reconstituted effort at modernizing schooling in Taiwan could be undertaken. It may be said that this new effort began with the adoption in 1954 of the Joint College Entrance Examination. This exam was designed for two purposes: to ensure the academic proficiency of students admitted to the university and to reduce the influence of family wealth on university admission. In short, the exam was an egalitarian move toward making merit, rather than money, the basis for continuing on to university studies.

The next major step toward education reform was the extension, in 1968, of compulsory schooling from grade six to grade nine. This moved more of the population closer to high school as an education goal. However, high schools continued to be designated either academic (college-bound, therefore elite) or vocational. Therefore another step toward egalitarianism was needed to boost the standing of those students who were tracked into vocational high schools. That step was the development of junior colleges.

The Junior College System

Junior colleges in Taiwan date back to the 1940s, but their development into a major component of the education system began in earnest in the 1960s. Even today, the number of students who attend junior colleges is relatively small. But the effect on Taiwan's economy and social structure has been profound.

I should note that K-12 education on Taiwan is highly regarded. The International Assessment of Educational Progress administered in 1994 by the Educational Testing Service (ETS) ranked Taiwan and Korea at the top of the list in science and math achievement by 13-year-olds. This is almost a contradiction, because the traditional emphases in Confucian education (the historical basis for Chinese education) are history, literature, and the arts. But, in fact, education as a whole is prized in Chinese culture; and perhaps that can be seen as the true foundation of education successes in Taiwan.

During the post-World War II period, much in Taiwanese education was taken from American school models. The development of the junior college system is both an extension and a permutation of this American influence.

Unlike American junior colleges, the Chinese junior colleges of Taiwan offer five-year programs and more closely resemble what have become known as "tech prep" programs in the United States. Today, 74 junior colleges in Taiwan enroll some 200,000 students in five-year programs (grades 10 to 14). The combined graduating classes in 1997 numbered approximately 35,000. However, junior colleges also enroll two-year students, as I will explain in a moment.

Tech Prep Taiwan-Style

I call this fastback *Tech Prep Taiwan-Style* because the junior college system in some ways mirrors the tech prep movement in U.S. education. The U.S. movement most often is termed a "2 + 2" program, in that it links the final two years of high school with two years of vocational, technical, or community college — i.e., junior college. In Taiwan linkage is less at issue. Instead, the junior college begins at what U.S. education would label grade 10 and continues for the next five years. Effectively, it might be said, this is a "3 + 2" program, seamlessly combining the final three years of high school with two years of college.

I mentioned previously that compulsory education was extended by law during the 1960s to nine years. This is termed the "national education" period. To continue past the ninth grade, a student must sit for a national examination during the summer following the ninth school year. With a rigidity not uncharacteristic of most Asian nations, this exam is "high stakes." The results will determine the young person's future, certainly in terms of further schooling and, in many cases, in terms of future employment as well.

Several paths exist, depending on the results of the examination. The most prestigious is to be admitted to an academic high school. This is the traditional college-bound path, and success on this path will lead to the university. About 40% of the students who sit for the annual exam pass on to an academic high school.

In the past the alternative to the academic high school was the vocational high school, a three-year high school that emphasized vocational/technical training. Vocational high school students were trained for practical trades, much as students in traditional U.S. vocational high schools are trained. Those students who could not qualify even for vocational high school passed on to other, shorter-term training — some public, some private — as auto mechanics, beauticians, cooks, and so on.

These vocational options still exist, but a great many students now opt for the junior college. In fact, about a quarter of the students who sit for the national exam after the ninth grade now enter 5-year junior colleges. Another 25% will enter a junior college after attending a vocational high school. The attendance and graduation figures I mentioned earlier are larger when both five- and two-year students are included. Combining these students, the junior colleges serve some 396,000 students and annually graduate more than 100,000.

Aspects of Egalitarianism

The junior college system in Taiwan provides thousands of men and women with the opportunity to attain the skills and credentials that will allow them to earn higher incomes and achieve higher social status than was the case in the past when the junior college option either did not exist or was more limited.

Education is a high priority in Taiwan. Of the 23 million citizens of the modern Republic of China, some 5,230,000 are involved in some form of education. About 753,000 (as of 1995) were involved in some form of higher education.

Students who enter a five-year junior college program are not faced with remedial education. The national examination ensures that the students are competent on a level equivalent to the 10th grade. It should not be construed that the students entering a five-year junior college program are comparable to U.S. students entering junior college after high school graduation. But, whereas many U.S. junior colleges are viewed as inferior in quality to four-year institutions, the Taiwanese junior colleges carry great academic prestige.

To capture the essence of the Chinese junior college, it should be remembered that the student entering a junior college after ninth grade usually is about 16 years old. He or she will likely graduate at the age of 21 or 22. This makes the student slightly older than his or her American contemporary, the result of a slightly later starting age for students entering first grade in Taiwan than in most U.S. communities.

Another egalitarian aspect of the junior college system is availability. Junior colleges can be found in most small cities throughout Taiwan. The larger urban areas, such as Taipei, Kaoshiung, Taichung, Tainan, Keelung, and Hualin, have several facilities in each city. In the beginning most of the junior colleges were public institutions, but private junior colleges began to appear during the 1960s. The private colleges now outnumber the public ones. However, all aspects of the junior colleges — curriculum, admission standards, faculty hiring, administrator placement, and so on — are overseen by the national Ministry of Education and by the provincial department of education.

A further aspect of junior college egalitarianism is the ethnic/racial makeup of the student body. The population of Taiwan is composed of three groups: native Taiwanese, mainland immigrants, and aborigines. Natives of Taiwan may be defined as those Chinese who came to the island mainly between the 14th and 19th centuries. Later Chinese immigrants are post-Chinese civil war arrivals, those who fled the Communists in the 1940s and 1950s. The smallest but most diverse group of Taiwan citizens is the aborigines. The aborigines comprise eight Polynesian tribal groups who migrated, in some cases as much as 10,000 years ago, from Malaysia, the Philippines, and other islands.

Of the 23 million people in Taiwan, about 19 million belong to the first group. Another 3.5 million trace more recent roots to mainland China, and the remainder are aborigines. A roughly proportional distribution can be found in the junior college student population with one notable exception: Aboriginal people are significantly under-represented in the junior college system and in all areas of secondary and postsecondary education.

Signs of Success

One of the most positive aspects of the junior college system is its low attrition rate. Few students who are admitted to a junior college fail to complete their studies. Indeed, only about 10% of the students drop out, most giving reasons such as family or financial problems, adjustment problems, poor health, or the irresistible lure of a job opportunity.

During my research in Taiwan I asked students why they chose to go into a five-year junior college program. Their answers almost invariably related to employment. Ninety percent said that they wanted to be able to find a good job and make a decent living for themselves and their families. The second most-mentioned reason was to please their parents by continuing their education. The third reason was simply that they could not qualify for a place in an academic high school and so wanted the next best thing. The fourth reason was to continue school life and friendships. And the fifth reason was that they hoped to use the five-year junior college as a launch pad for university studies.

This last reason warrants a comment. Just as few students drop out of junior college, it also is true that few graduate from the five-year program and go on to a university. To make this leap, the student must pass a difficult admission exam. If successful, the student will be admitted, in all likelihood, as a sophomore with little credit given for the junior college experience. When I asked officials at the Ministry of Education about this situation, they indicated that junior college does not typically prepare a student for the highly competitive university entrance exam. Beyond that, it should be said that few students make the attempt, a fact that education officials attribute to most students' expectation of entering the job market following attainment of the five-year junior college diploma.

The latter is particularly true for males. Females appear to be far more likely to continue into a university education after graduating from a junior college than male students, in the main because they are less likely to depend on getting a good job and supporting a family in traditional Chinese society.

This situation has given rise to discussion in Taiwan's education circles. The question has been raised with regard to how the brightest junior college graduates can be encouraged (or enticed) to continue their education at a university without imposing a financial burden or unreasonably extending the time that it takes to earn a bachelor's degree.

Finally, one unmistakable sign of success for the junior college system is the economic advantage it gives to graduates. The student who completes only the compulsory national education of nine years will likely earn about half as much as the student who goes on to high school but completes only 11 years of school. The high school graduate will earn twice as much as the high school dropout. But the junior college graduate will likely earn twice as much as the high school graduate. Clearly, education makes a difference financially. And the difference between junior college graduation and matriculation at a four-year university is not as great as between a high school graduate and a junior college graduate, though the university graduate will likely earn about 60% more than the junior college graduate.

Perhaps as important to most Chinese students is the satisfaction that comes from achieving a junior college certificate. In Chinese society, academic achievement has always been tied to job satisfaction and social standing, as well as to economic benefit. The five-year junior college system has given many students opportunities to raise their social standing and to enhance their job satisfaction — opportunities that did not exist (or existed for very few) prior to the 1960s.

A Day in the Life

To an extent, the junior colleges in Taiwan extend childhood, or at least the version of childhood that one finds in Taiwanese elementary and secondary schools. Students who attend junior colleges are required to wear uniforms, be appropriately groomed, and behave in a respectful manner. The students seldom miss a class unless they are seriously ill or have a family emergency. Discipline problems are few. The students socialize before and after school, but dating, public displays of affection, smoking, fighting, and boisterous behavior in general are treated as inappropriate.

Dating is specifically discouraged during the first three years of junior college; however, in the last two years students may participate in a variety of coed activities, such as attending movies, going to parties, and going out to dinner. Behaving inappropriately while in uniform can bring negative consequences. Each uniform displays information about the student above the left-hand breast pocket of the shirt or jacket. This information not only identifies the student's school, but also the student by name and identification number. The misbehaving student can be identified and reported to school authorities, even during off-school hours.

Expulsion is the most dire punishment, not only because it deprives the student of needed schooling, but also because it carries a serious social stigma and, in fact, can damage the student's future job opportunities. When I interviewed students at Kwang-Wu Junior College, they unanimously confirmed the importance of proper behavior and could recall no one among their comrades who had been sent away for misbehavior. Incidentally, Kwang-Wu Junior College is fairly representative of Chinese junior colleges. It has about 7,000 students. Only about 100 drop out of school in any given year, most because of health problems, family crises, injuries (often related to traffic accidents in the Taipei area), or because they transfer to a university abroad after their third year.

Admission Procedures

I have stated previously that admission to a five-year junior college is based on an exam that students take on completion of the nine years of compulsory education. The exam process is staged. The exam for admission to an academic high school, which will put the student on the university track, is conducted in July. Students' scores arrive within two weeks. If the student is unsuccessful at qualifying for a place in an academic high school, then he or she may register for the junior college exam, which is held in August. All of this makes for a stressful summer; but by the start of the new school year every student knows the path that he or she will be taking for the next few years and, in fact, where that path is likely to lead in terms of career and social status.

The junior college admission exam concentrates on four areas: Chinese (language and literature), mathematics, natural sciences, and social sciences. This last category includes Chinese history, geography, and politics; San Min Chu-yi ("Three Principles of the People"); and English. The score achieved on the junior college admission exam will determine not only whether the student will be admitted to a junior college, but which college the student will attend. Chinese junior colleges are ranked according to their status, and students who score highest are given places in the highest ranked colleges.

The most prestigious junior college is National Taipei Junior College, which is heavily funded by city government, has an excellent faculty, and charges very low tuition. This college has a distinguished record of placing its graduates into high-paying positions, and a significant number of the graduates matriculate into universities in Taiwan and abroad.

Public and private junior college tuition varies. The public institutions charge between US$1,000 and US$1,200 annually. The private institutions tend to charge more. For example, Kwang-Wu Junior College charges a tuition of about US$3,000 each year. The average per capita income in Taiwan in 1999 is about US$11,500.

Academic Life

Admission to an academic high school presupposes a desire for matriculation to a university, and so the mission of the academic high school is for students to qualify for university admission — in other words, to pass yet another admission exam. The mission of the five-year junior college is very different.

Because the five-year program is seen as an end in itself, the atmosphere of the typical junior college is much more relaxed and competition-free than the academic high school. In short, the junior college student need never face another high-stress exam unless he or she is in the minority of students that plans to transfer to the university after graduating from the junior college. This "closed-end" view of the junior college experience is expressed in a dual-component curriculum. One component is academic preparation; the other is professional, or career, preparation.

The academic component is not unlike the curriculum of the academic high school. Junior college students are required to take classes in mathematics, the sciences, computer science, Chinese, and English, just as their academic high school counterparts do. The subjects become more challenging each year. For example, in mathematics study progresses from algebra to geometry and trigonometry to calculus and math theory.

The lecture predominates as an instructional method, particularly during the first three years of junior college. Classes are coeducational, and each class during these years includes about 35 students. Classrooms are quiet. Students stand as the instructor enters the room, and the class leader (usually a student with excellent grades, elected by his or her classmates) acknowledges the teacher's presence. Then the students sit down. Most students take few notes, preferring instead to rely on their textbooks and workbooks. They tend to jot notes in the margins of those books.

In a few classes, the lecture method gives way to demonstration teaching, such as in the sciences and physical education. Language classes and classes in the social sciences often use small-group discussion. Some classes use a seminar approach: The students are given an assignment, break into small groups, and then reconvene to report back to the teacher. This method of instruction is unusual in Chinese education and so tends not to be very successful, according to my observation. Chinese elementary and junior high schools tend to emphasize rote learning, and students often are conditioned to passivity rather than initiative.

Students are encouraged to keep a journal of their academic activities and to keep a comprehensive calendar of required assignments, dates due, and other matters. Journals, workbooks, and assignments are reviewed regularly. Students who fail to complete assignments or do shoddy work often are publicly reprimanded by their instructors. This results in a loss of face, a serious matter, and tends to discourage poor performance.

Quizzes are frequent but not regarded as very important. Each school year is divided into four terms, and it is the term-end, comprehensive tests that are important. These quarterly exams determine whether a student may move forward to the next level of study.

The professional component is introduced during the first three years of junior college but stressed during the last two. For example, a student studying chemical or electronic engineering likely will take only one or two classes in this field during the first three years. However, during the fourth and fifth years more than half of his or her study time will be devoted to the specialization.

Students also may "explore" during the first three years of junior college; but by what would be termed grade 13, they should firmly decide on a "major," or field of concentration. Many options exist, including computers, electronic engineering, mechanical engineering, business and commerce, international trade, language studies, chemistry, medical technology, physical therapy, nursing, and so on. The choice of a field of concentration will determine the nature of the classwork. Students majoring in chemistry, for example, will spend most of their time not in lectures but in laboratories.

Junior colleges also are differentiated by the majors they are able to offer. For example, Kwang-Wu Junior College in Taipei concentrates on majors in chemistry, computers, electronic engineering, international trade, electronic machine design, mechanical engineering, and foreign languages. Taipei Junior College in the same city focuses on business administration, accounting, banking, and finance. Wen Tzao Junior College in southern Taiwan emphasizes foreign languages.

Because fields of concentration are determined on the basis of exam scores for admission, I was interested in how satisfied students were with their school, teachers, subjects, and social life. I unsystematically chose 120 interview subjects spread across all five years of junior college and posed the question. Eighty percent said they were "very satisfied" with their schooling and social life; 15% were "moderately satisfied"; and 5% were disappointed either because their expectations had not been met or they felt that the school was not providing adequate training in their chosen field. These dissatisfied students, on the whole, seemed to feel as though they would have been satisfied had they chosen a different field of study.

The Schedule

The junior college school year is about 240 days long, beginning in August and ending in July. However, there are numerous holidays sprinkled throughout the year. Major breaks are the Chinese New Year and a spring vacation. October and November tend to have the greatest number of three-day weekends, no doubt because the country's patriotic holidays also fall in those months. The school week is Monday through Saturday.

Typically, students arrive at the college about eight o'clock and go to a "homeroom," where they leave their knapsacks or attaché cases. They wear uniforms that are gray, blue, black, or khaki, depending on the junior college they attend. Male students wear white shirts and ties; females wear light-colored blouses. Uniforms are considered to be important because they remove economic status visibility. Students from poor families are indistinguishable from students from wealthy families. But the uniforms themselves convey status; they show that the student has been accepted at a particular junior college.

About 8:20 classes begin. The first class lasts about 45 minutes, followed by a 10- or 15-minute break. During the break students can go into the institution's court-yard and socialize. The next class then starts, and the pattern is followed throughout the day. Occasionally, the class schedule is interrupted for an assembly of some type. For example, students studying engineering might be gathered to hear a professional engineer talk about the profession.

The academic day is interrupted by lunch, and most students eat in college lunchrooms and purchase their meals there. A typical lunch might include soup, rice, chicken or fish, three or four green vegetables, and a se-lection of fruit. Tea is available in some lunchrooms, but many colleges expect students to bring their own bev-erages from home. Junior college lunch facilities are clean, and the food is well-prepared. Lunch prices range from US$1 to US$1.50, and second servings of rice and soup are always available. Because of the large number of students to be served, lunch hours at most junior col-leges are staggered around midday.

In some smaller colleges a 15-minute post-lunch pe-riod is scheduled for students to nap at their desks. This is a common tradition in many Asian societies and seems to re-energize both faculty (who nap in the staff room) and students. The larger junior colleges do not follow this tradition.

Classes end about 4:20 in the afternoon. Again, now and then, a major speaker will be reason to call the students together for a final assembly of 15 or 20 min-utes. Most assemblies are held in the college's central courtyard, a feature of almost all such institutions. The courtyard also is used for students to socialize, exercise, and relax.

Sports and exercise are encouraged at the college. Recreation includes playing volleyball, soccer, badminton, table tennis, Frisbee, and football; but the most popular is basketball. Incidental recreation is taken up throughout the day. Organized sports are conducted after the 4:20 dismissal of classes.

By about 6:30 in the evening, junior college students have arrived at home. Although most student will have some homework, the homework demands of junior college are significantly less than those of either the junior high school (grades 7-9) or the highly competitive academic high school. Most junior college instructors assign homework daily, but many students complete their work at the college in a study hall.

A small percentage (only about 25%) of junior college students hold part-time jobs. The jobs are typical of students everywhere: fast-food restaurants, delivery services, gas stations, and family-owned businesses. Junior college attendance carries status such that parents seldom expect that their children will work outside of school.

Night School

Virtually all junior colleges in Taiwan operate both a day school and a night school. Most of what I have said so far applies to the day school. Incidentally, I should mention that on Saturdays the same 8:00 a.m. to 4:20 p.m. schedule is followed as on weekdays. Admission to the day school is more demanding than admission to the night school, which is designed for students who need and want further schooling but may not be able to pass the standard junior college admission exam.

Night school students attend classes from about 6:20 until 10:40 each weekday evening, but they do not have classes on Saturdays (though they make up that time in other ways). The curriculum for night school students is approximately the same as for day students. Because the evening classes are shorter than the day classes, night school students will attend more days of the year than day students in order to equalize the time. Recreational and sports opportunities, however, will be fewer for the night school students.

Taiwan remains a relatively safe environment for students to travel between home and college, whether by day or by evening. A public bus system extends throughout the island, including rural areas, and is heavily used by junior college students. Many other students ride bicycles or motorcycles, and a few from affluent families may be allowed to use the family car. However, the use of private cars is discouraged because parking spaces are hard to find.

Sadly, there has been some increase in recent years in students being attacked while in transit to or from evening classes. Females are most often the victims of such attacks, and the government has stepped up efforts to keep students safe. However, compared to the violence found in urban areas in the United States, Taiwan's cities and suburban areas are very safe.

Faculties and Facilities

I mentioned previously that all junior colleges, public and private, are governed by the Ministry of Education, which also is true for all other education institutions. The curricula of the public and private institutions is approximately the same. The public institutions generally are regarded as higher in prestige than the private colleges, and they are better funded. The private junior colleges must charge higher tuition than the public institutions, but they still cannot match the funding level of the public colleges. Consequently, public junior colleges can offer larger libraries, smaller classes, and better-paid teachers than the private institutions can. For example, the teacher-student ratio at a public institution is likely to be about 1:15, while at a private junior college the ratio may be 1:20.

The main leadership of a junior college rests with a principal, assistant principal, director of finance, director of curriculum, director of discipline and moral development, and director of military science. Academic departments are led by a chairperson, often the senior teacher in the department. Most faculty members in the junior colleges hold at least a baccalaureate degree; about 40% hold a master's degree; and a few hold a doctorate. Individuals with very specialized skills who do not hold a college degree may be hired on a part-time basis to teach at a junior college.

Over the past half-century junior college faculty composition has changed dramatically. Today, about 33% of junior college teachers are women, compared to only 7% in 1950, when the junior college system was just starting to develop. Instructors at the junior college level are referred to as "professor." Ranks begin with "teaching assistant," a person with specialized skills who may or may not yet have earned a bachelor's degree. If the individual does not yet hold a degree, he or she will continue to work toward that goal while employed at the junior college. The next rank is "lecturer" (or "instructor"), usually a person with a master's degree who has served as a teaching assistant for a period of time.

Six years of experience as a lecturer and a doctorate are required to move to the rank of "associate professor," though this rank can be achieved by exceptional individuals who hold only a master's degree. Significant publications, research skills, and recommendations from colleagues count heavily in the promotion decision.

The highest rank in the junior college faculty system is "professor." To become a professor, one must have been an associate professor for at least three years and be able to present an array of professional publications for review by the junior college faculty and the Ministry of Education. A doctorate is required but, again, exceptions may be made for exceptional individuals.

Classroom and laboratory facilities at the junior colleges are similar to those found in other developed countries. Libraries, however, tend to be small. The typical library collection includes professional books and journals, encyclopedias, and other standard items; but works of literature and philosophy, books in foreign languages, and works intended for leisure reading are not usually included.

The junior college student pays about US$400 each year for textbooks, which are the main source of required reading. The textbooks are standardized by the Ministry of Education, and few originate outside Taiwan, with one exception. Most textbooks are rather plain paperbacks, often accompanied by a workbook; a single class may require several such sets. The students carry their books to class each day, usually in large knapsacks.

The exception to Chinese textbooks is the use of English-language, specifically American, textbooks for certain subjects. I noticed this curious feature when I visited several junior colleges. Students often could be seen using American textbooks in classes for math, science, engineering, chemistry, biology, and several other subjects. When I asked principals and teachers about this, I was told that such use resulted from a couple of reasons. First, the American textbooks were more up-to-date than those available in Chinese; and, second, it was too expensive to have the American books translated into Chinese. Certainly, the use of English-language textbooks must be challenging for junior college students; but such a challenge also may serve to reinforce the students' study of English, which is a required subject in Taiwan schools from early on.

I have said that the classroom facilities would look familiar to most students in developed countries. However, there are unique aspects to the Chinese junior college campus. Almost universally, the campuses are walled compounds. (Incidentally, this is true of most education institutions.) The main entrance to the campus is a front gate supervised by a uniformed security guard. The wall serves both practical and symbolic purposes. Its practical purpose is security, but equally important is its symbolic purpose of setting apart the learning institution from the "outside world." The wall emphasizes the importance of education.

The campuses I visited were all well-kept. Inside the wall the grounds were beautifully landscaped and immaculate. Students, faculty, and all who work within the campus compound seem to take deep pride in their environment, whether the campus is small or large.

Graduation

Junior college students need 220 credits in order to graduate after five years. This number, like the curriculum, is established by the Ministry of Education. I noted previously that the first three years of junior college (equivalent to the last three years of high school) are virtually identical in all institutions. And the curriculum at this time roughly parallels that of a typical academic high school. Students take classes in Chinese, English, mathematics, the sciences, computer science, and social studies. A few students supplement their regular classroom work by attending "bushi-ban." Bushi-ban are after-school classes taught by professional educators who supplement their income by tutoring small groups of students. English is a primary subject for bushi-ban. I was curious about this fact; and so during my interviews with junior college students, I asked, "Why English?" Two reasons predominated. First, many students believe that they will have a future opportunity to travel to the United States, either for advanced study or for employment. Second, English often is considered the most difficult subject in the Chinese junior college, and students are required to pass it in order to graduate.

By the end of the fifth year, junior college students are in their early 20s. Graduation time brings new decisions: Should they seek employment? Should they continue their education through a specialized training program, such as advanced training in the sciences or computers? Or should they try for admission to the university? Most students choose the first path and seek employment. The motivation for this move is primarily economic. But increasingly students are opting either for more specialized training or for admission to a university.

The latter course, I have suggested, is a difficult one. But the Ministry of Education in recent years has begun to set up mechanisms to make it easier. Nowadays, for example, a graduating junior college student can sit for an exam that, if passed, will allow the student to enter the university as a sophomore rather than as a freshman.

For graduating students who do not plan to go for further training or a university degree, the junior college administration assists with finding employment. Male students, however, may postpone job searching in favor of fulfilling their 20-month military service obligation. That obligation is set aside for male students who enter a university; however, as I noted previously, the junior college-to-university transition is made in disproportionately higher numbers by females.

The goal of the Ministry of Education is to place greater emphasis on junior college education, along with other alternatives to the university. I stated previously that about 40% of students move from junior high school into a university-track academic high school. The

Ministry of Education would like to see this number reduced to about 35%, and the percentage of students who go on to a junior college or some other form of continuing education to rise to about 65%, up from some 50% of students at the present time.

Critical Analysis

The junior college system in Taiwan has had, and will continue to have, a powerful effect on education generally, the economy, and social mobility. While it is not without flaws, it is nonetheless highly successful. The five-year junior college in particular is without parallel in the United States, but it comes close to exemplifying one interpretation of the philosophy that undergirds the tech prep movement, which is to create a seamless transition from K-12 schooling to some form of higher or continuing education. For that reason alone, Western — particularly American — educators and policy makers may want to take a closer look at the Chinese junior college.

In terms of a critical analysis of the five-year junior college, it is not my purpose to find fault. But areas of both success and difficulty were pointed out to me at the five junior colleges where I made observations and conducted interviews in 1997. These areas are worth exploring briefly.

First, it must be said that the atmosphere at the colleges I visited was overwhelmingly positive. The campuses were attractive and well-maintained, the faculties were articulate and committed, and the students were motivated, well-groomed, and energetic. Thus it makes good sense to first take up the opportunities that are the great positives of the junior college system and, second, to address some of the criticisms that have been leveled at the system.

Opportunities

The junior college offers young men and women opportunities to further their education, to study subjects that will lead to good jobs, and to raise their social standing through education. Few students who enter a junior college will fail to complete the program of study, and 70% of junior college graduates immediately find work in their field on completing school. Opportunities for advancement in a chosen career and financial success are significantly improved for young workers who have completed a junior college education.

Many junior college graduates choose not to go on to a trade program or to the university, some, interestingly enough, because they intend to pursue a master's degree program outside Taiwan, in Japan, Australia, or the United States. The junior college experience builds confidence as well as competence.

The subjects of study available through the junior college system are many and wide-ranging. The five-year program builds a base of general knowledge similar to that provided by the more prestigious academic high school. On that base each student then constructs a professional competence that will translate directly into an entry-level job in a professional career. I previously listed examples of this range of subjects, and the range truly is wide.

Criticisms

Like most Asian education systems, the Chinese junior college contains elements of social rigidity. There is no provision for the inclusion of students who have had social or criminal problems during their early school years. Nor is there any provision for talented students to move from the junior college to the academic high school, though, as I have noted, some students can move to the university directly after completing junior college. Once the die has been cast by means of the admission exams, students are tied to their choice of an education path. As one student expressed it to me, "I feel locked in but believe that, if I had a chance to do it over again, I could have passed admission into the academic high school."

The junior college is lower in status than the academic high school that leads to university admission. In spite of a Confucian tradition that prizes all education, the "technical training" aspect of the junior college relegates even its rigorous education to a lesser status than the university-track high school.

Educators themselves have expressed concern that the five-year program is too long and includes redundancies in some coursework. One professor with whom I spoke suggested that the five-year program might be compressed into four years with automatic matriculation to a technical college; however, the main difficulty with implementing such a suggestion is the lack of technical colleges. It would be impossible to accommodate all of the graduates of the junior colleges in this way.

Another frustration expressed by some educators is the slowness with which the junior college is able to change and adapt to new technology, a serious handicap in a rapidly changing world. As one professor commented, "I learned computer science fifteen years ago, and I have tried to keep myself updated. The industries in Taiwan are moving more quickly than teachers understand. We simply have to spend all of our free time trying to keep up with the changes that are taking place in computers so that we can pass on the latest information to students."

A number of critics have charged that the junior college offers too little in the way of classes in music, art, philosophy, drama, and literature. Compliance with the academic requirements of the Ministry of Education and the technical and commercial requirements of the industries of Taiwan make it very difficult for the average student to gain a broad exposure to the humanities. The only way to solve this problem would be to include more such classes in the curriculum. However, doing so could adversely affect the existing academic and technical training.

Finally, perhaps the most insightful criticism was shared with me by officials in the Ministry of Education, as well as by junior college faculty and administrators. Many students, they pointed out, simply do not know what career they want to pursue. After all, the students are channeled by the exams into a particular path at the age of 16, long before many young men and women have any clear idea about their future in the workplace and society. Yet few students are able to make any dramatic change of career direction, in spite of minor "exploration" opportunities early in the five-year experience.

At the same time, it must be said that such a system increases the stability of the junior college system. For example, it allows greater certainty in planning the number of faculty needed in certain fields, the number of prospective graduates into certain segments of the job market, and so on. And the possibility of changing majors is not entirely removed by the system. Students can take an "internal transfer examination" and change majors, though this course of action is discouraged.

Positives on Which to Build

The Chinese junior college system offers many opportunities, opportunities that did not exist for the parents and grandparents of many of today's students. But the junior college system, as I have pointed out, is not without its critics; and many of the criticisms are well-founded. Nevertheless, there are significant positives on which the junior college system may build for the future.

Of the 74 junior colleges in Taiwan, a majority are private institutions controlled by individual boards of trustees that operate under rules established by the Ministry of Education. These rules ensure that each junior college is set on an adequate parcel of land, has a sound financial base (the Ministry provides a small amount of funding), and offers subjects that meet the needs of their students. Although tuition is higher at the private junior colleges (as much as US$3,000 a semester compared to US$1,000 at the public institutions), the difference between the two is not overwhelming.

Boards of trustees do not involve themselves with the day-to-day operation of the private junior colleges. Their main task is to hire the college president and oversee his or her work. Private junior college presidents normally are distinguished educators with three-year, renewable appointments. The public junior colleges — there are 19 — are operated much like the national universities. Their presidents are appointed by the Ministry of Education, which, much like the private boards of trustees, does not get involved in day-to-day operations. Thus at both private and public institutions, educators are left to determine matters best left to educators. In observing both types of institution, I found little to differentiate them in terms of quality of schooling.

Conclusion

Taiwan, like all modern nations, is facing rapid industrial and technological change. Such change also is reflected in changes in family life: more abuse, more divorce, but also more leisure time, more disposable income. How does this bear on the junior college?

Parent involvement in junior college education is almost nonexistent. No general parent-teacher organization concept exists in Taiwan. Parents may step in to help their children obtain tutoring, particularly in English and mathematics; but, beyond that, they are little connected to their children's educational experience beyond the ninth grade. In other words, the junior college, even though it includes what would be considered 10th, 11th, and 12th grades, is *college*, not high school.

Recognizing this, the junior colleges have stepped in to fill the void. All of the junior college campuses I visited provide excellent counseling services for young adults experiencing family, emotional, or psychological problems. In addition, junior colleges are required by law to provide health services on campus for their students. Doctors, nurses, and dentists are readily available to assist students.

The Ministry of Education provides strong, unified guidance to Taiwan's junior college system. It is not a system in stagnation. Rather, it is a system in development, constantly improving. From its beginnings half a century ago, the junior college system has consistently worked toward better serving the needs of its students. As a result, it has proven to be effective in raising levels of education, income, and status for many in Taiwan.

Resources

Following are a number of resources for additional reading about education in Taiwan and related matters.

Amsden, Alice. "The State and Taiwan's Economic Development." In *Bring the State Back*, edited by Peter Evans. New York: Cambridge University Press, 1986.

Chin, Robert, and Chin, Ai-Li. "Comparative Evaluations of Aspects of Contemporary Chinese Culture by College Students in Taiwan." *National Taiwan University Journal of Sociology* 23 (December 1983): 41-57.

Chiu, Hwi-yuan. "Education and Social Change in Taiwan." In *Taiwan: A New Industrialized State*, edited by H.H. Hsiao, W.Y. Cheng, and H.S. Chan. Taipei: National Taiwan University Press, 1989.

Clark, Cal. "Economic Development in Taiwan." *Journal of Asian and African Studies* No. 22 (1987): 1-6.

Education Statistical Indicators: Republic of China. Taipei: Ministry of Education, 1997.

Education: The Republic of China. Taipei: Bureau of Statistics, Ministry of Education, 1997.

Fairbank, John K.; Reischauer, Edwin O.; and Craig, Albert M. *East Asia: Tradition and Transformation*. Boston: Houghton Mifflin, 1973.

Gabel, Thomas. *State and Society: The Taiwan Miracle*. Armonk, N.Y.: M.E. Sharpe, 1986.

Hou, Chi-Ming, and Chang, Ching-Hsi. "Education and Economic Growth in Taiwan." In *Experience and Lessons of Economic Development in Taiwan*, edited by K.T. Li and T.S. Yen. Taipei: Academia Sinica, 1982. (in Chinese)

Hsiung, James C., ed. *The Taiwan Experience, 1950-1980*. New York: American Association for Chinese Studies, 1981.

Ignas, Edward, et. al. *Comparative Educational Systems*. Chicago: F.E. Peacock, 1981.

Introduction to Technological and Vocational Educations of the Republic of China. Taipei: Department of Technological Education, Ministry of Education, 1996.

Jackson, M. Robert. "The Role of Higher Education in the Realization of the National Goals of the Republic of China." Doctoral dissertation, Arizona State University, 1971.

Kwang-Wu Junior College of Technology: 20 Year Review. Taipei: College Publishers, 1994. (in Chinese)

Lew, William J.F. "Education in Taiwan: Trends and Problems." *Asian Affairs* 3 (May 1978): 317-22.

Liu, Chien, and Armer, J. Michael. "Education's Effect on Economic Growth in Taiwan." *Comparative Education Review* 37 (August 1993): 303-32.

National Taipei Junior College of Business: An Introduction. Taipei: College Press, 1994.

Prospectus: Kwang-Wu Institute of Technology and Commerce. Taipei: College Press, 1997.

Shih, Paul K.T., ed. *Taiwan in Modern Times*. New York: St. John's University Press, 1973.

Smith, Douglas C. *The Dewey-Confucius Synthesis: Higher Education in Taiwan*. Taipei: Academic Press and U.S. Department of Education, 1978.

Smith, Douglas C. "Higher Education in Taiwan." *Journal of the West Virginia Historical Association* 10 (Spring 1979): 1-53.

Smith, Douglas C. *An Island of Learning: Academeocracy in Taiwan*. Taipei: Pacific Cultural Foundation, 1981.

Smith, Douglas C. "Competitive Examinations." *China Review* (August 1982): 23-31.

Smith, Douglas C. *In the Image of Confucius: The Preparation and Education of Teachers in Taiwan*. Reprint. Washington, D.C.: U.S. Department of Education, ERIC Center, 1984.

Smith, Douglas C. "The Confucian Legacy: Traditions in Modern Chinese Education." In *Confucianism and the Modern World*, edited by Li-Fu Chen. Taipei: The Confucius-Mencius Society of China, 1988.

Smith, Douglas C. "Chinese Education and Modern Taiwan: An Eidetic Interpretation." *Tunghai Journal of Humanities* 4 (1988): 215-31.

Smith, Douglas C. *The Confucian Continuum: Educational Modernization in Taiwan*. New York: Praeger, 1991.

Smith, Douglas C. "Redesigning Education: The Elevation of Teacher Education in Taiwan, China, 1982-1992." *Asian Quarterly* 22, no. 2 (1994): 15-30.

Wilson, Richard. *Learning to Be Chinese. The Political Socialization of Children in Taiwan*. Cambridge, Mass.: MIT Press, 1970.